SpongeBob™ SquarePants

NICKELODEON®

illustrated by Caleb Muerer

You may think you know everything about **SpongeBob SquarePants,** but there's more to this unsinkable yellow sea sponge than meets the eye. For instance, did you know it takes a whole **team of animators** to bring SpongeBob—and the rest of the **Bikini Bottom** bunch—to your television screen? No kidding! After all, it takes 24 drawings to fill each second of an animated cartoon! And animators have to be certain the drawings are going to work together so their **characters seem lifelike.** It sounds like a lot of work, but animators have discovered some really nifty ways of making their jobs easier—and making **animation fun!** (Don't you just love shortcuts?) And with the help of the simple animation techniques explained in this book, you too can learn to create nautical nonsense from your own imagination in no time!

Are you ready-eddy-eddy?

Walk Underwater

The drawings on each odd-numbered page make up an **action cycle** of SpongeBob running. To view the action, hold the bound edge of the book and use your thumb to quickly flip the pages from back to front. (Directions for making your own flip book are on pages 28–29.)

What is "Animation"?

Animation brings a cartoon character to life. The character can be anything: a person, an animal, or an object. Animators draw characters like SpongeBob in successive positions (one following the next) to create movement, such as walking, running, waving, or talking. Then they add facial expressions to make the action more realistic. This book will show you how to animate some of Bikini Bottom's most popular residents. And along the way, you'll soak up helpful tips and information about the animation process. Are ya' ready, kids? Dive right in!

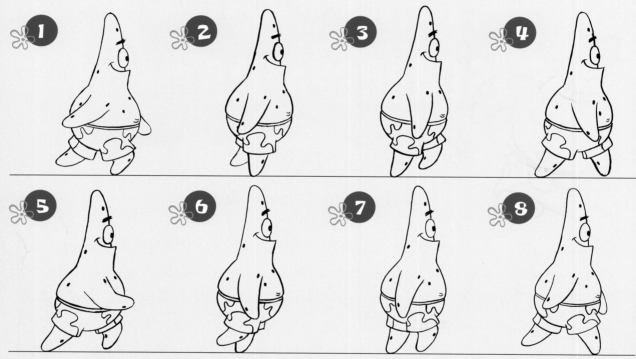

Bursting at the gills to get started? Let's begin by looking at a simple walk cycle. Notice that each new pose follows the action of the one before. Drawing 1 follows drawing 8 to continue the action, creating a cycle. To keep Patrick on the move, repeat the cycle. (See page 14 for more on cycles.)

Uno, Dos, Trace!

A **light box** is a glass-topped drawing table with a light inside. When the light shines through the glass, you can see through layers of paper. You can use a light box to trace images as you sketch one frame after another, which will help keep your characters consistent. And "animation pegs" at the bottom of the box anchor your prepunched paper in place. All you have to do is turn on the light—and trace away! (You can buy a light box at an art and craft store.)

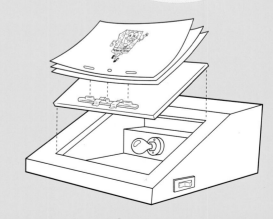

2

Tools and Materials

All you need to get started is a pencil, an eraser, a sharpener, and some bond or tracing paper. But as you can see below, there are a few other tools that will come in handy. Once you gather your supplies, you'll be animating SpongeBob and all his underwater buddies before you can say, "Krusty Krab Krabby Patties!"

Tracing paper
(or bond paper)

Eraser

Drawing
pencil

Sharpener

Black felt-tip pen

TiP
If you dont have a
light box, you can tape
your drawings to a
window and let the
sun shine through!

Drop-out pencils

A Few Extras

As your skills develop, you might want to pick up a few "extra" supplies. For example, animators use blue or red "drop-out" pencils to make rough sketches; then they draw the final, black lines over them with a felt-tip pen. (They also use the felt-tip pen to fill in details.) When the drawings are done, they're scanned into a computer, and special animation software causes the colored lines to "drop out" so that they don't print.

Square One

Before you can draw a character in action (which requires many, many drawings), you have to be able to draw the character from any angle and in any position. But don't let that scare you: Animators don't draw the entire character all at once; they take it one step at a time! And there's no better place to begin practicing than square one: drawing the basic shapes that make up a character's body. Start with the example below, which shows how to sketch SpongeBob, beginning with a simple square, plus guidelines that help you place his features. Then try drawing SpongeBob's basic shape from lots of different angles, following the examples on page 5.

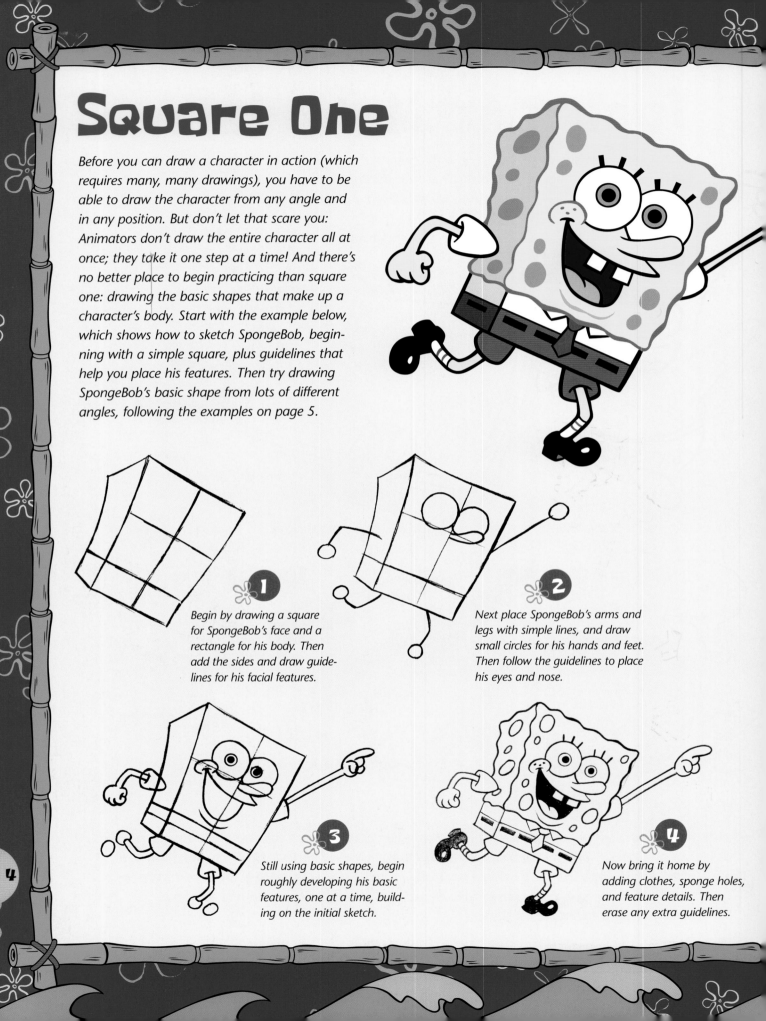

1 Begin by drawing a square for SpongeBob's face and a rectangle for his body. Then add the sides and draw guidelines for his facial features.

2 Next place SpongeBob's arms and legs with simple lines, and draw small circles for his hands and feet. Then follow the guidelines to place his eyes and nose.

3 Still using basic shapes, begin roughly developing his basic features, one at a time, building on the initial sketch.

4 Now bring it home by adding clothes, sponge holes, and feature details. Then erase any extra guidelines.

Busy Bodies

Now you're ready to work with SpongeBob's nautical neighbors. Want to be a shoe-in for "animator of the month"? Put in plenty of practice, and learn to draw each character from every angle—and in different poses.

1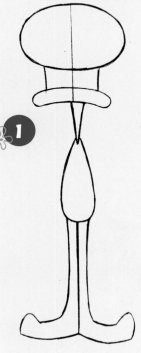

2

3

Squidward Tentacles

1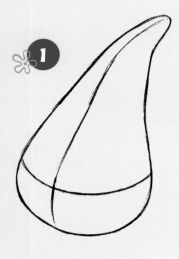

2

3

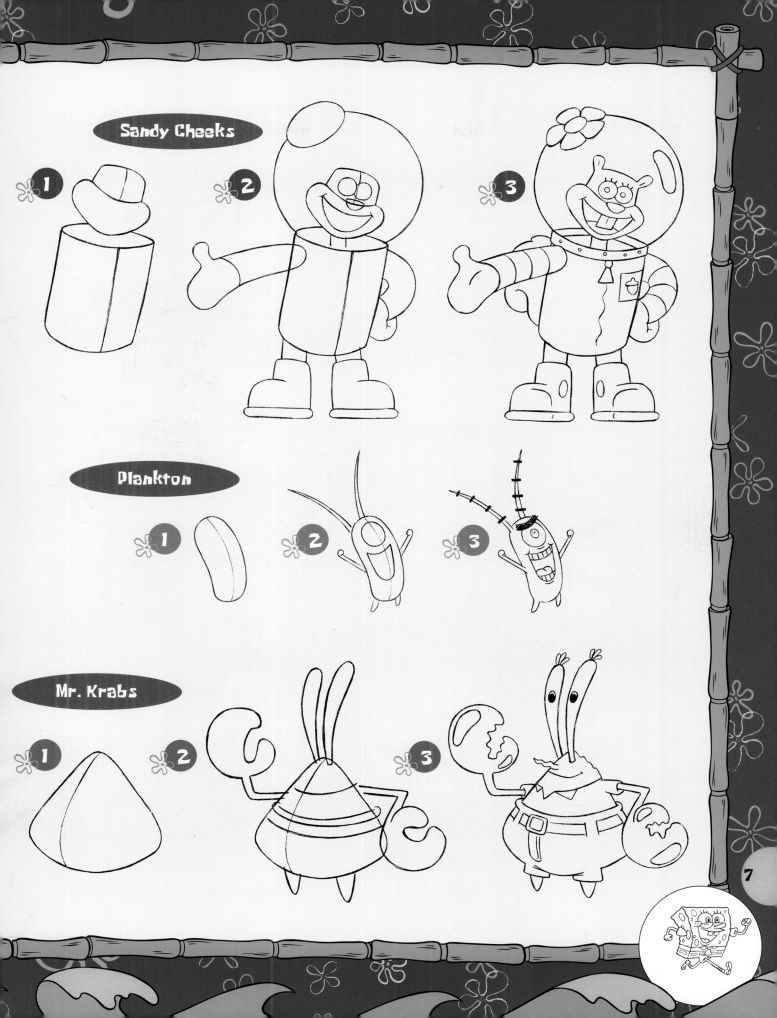

Sandy Cheeks

1 2 3

Plankton

1 2 3

Mr. Krabs

1 2 3

7

Wave of Emotion

Cartoon characters go through an ocean of emotions, from silly to shy. So how do you draw SpongeBob when he's hinga dinga dergin happy?! The easiest way to draw emotions is to first practice acting them out while looking at your face in a mirror. When you're excited, do your eyes and mouth open wide? Does your nose scrunch up with anticipation? Remember these details when you draw your character—then exaggerate them for emphasis! Some of SpongeBob's many emotional states are shown below.

| Content | Shy | Embarrassed | Stunned |

| Cranky | Scared | Flabbergasted | Worried |

SpongeBob isn't the only character whose expressions are exaggerated. In animation, extreme expressions (and poses!) really impact the viewer. SpongeBob's Bikini Bottom friends make it easy to understand how they're feeling because they always "go big" with their emotions!

Thrilled

Drowsy

Sneaky

Frustrated

Eager

Frightened

Giggly

Excited

Aggressive

Fuming

9

"Squash and Stretch"

When an expression or a movement needs to be exaggerated, a character will **stretch** to cartoon proportions to show it. But before this extreme action, there's a moment of anticipation when the character draws back, or **squashes.** Notice that when you use squash and stretch, some areas of the character's face and body don't change much at all—and other areas change a lot!

Here the pull of the fishhook is causing SpongeBob to stretch. Notice that his body (which is spongy) stretches out a lot, but his square pants stay pretty much the same shape and size.

You can also use the "squash" technique to show the weight of an object, as in this example of a heavy rock squashing Squidward's head.

When characters run, there is always some squash and stretch involved. In these two examples of SpongeBob and Patrick, the effect is obvious, as Patrick is stretched while SpongeBob is squashed (above), and vice versa (left).

10

"The Take"

Squash and stretch are an important part of the cartoon "take." A **take** is an exaggerated reaction to something a character sees (like a smelly swarm of anchovies arriving at the Krusty Krab) or experiences (like a painful jellyfish sting). Whether the character is reacting with surprise, fear, or glee, the take follows a few general rules. The character always anticipates the reaction, preparing with a squash. And the extreme action—the take—always involves wild stretching. After the take, the character returns to normal, or at least as close to "normal" as Bikini Bottom personalities get!

At the beginning, SpongeBob is just casually taking an undersea stroll.

Suddenly SpongeBob spots something fishy—a coin, smack in the middle of the street!

Next his body squashes to prepare for the big reaction to come—the take.

Now here's the take. He lifts off the ground and stretches, eyes bugging out and mouth open wide.

SpongeBob begins to recover, landing back on the ground with a subtle squash.

Kah-rah-tay! Action

The **line of action** is an imaginary guide for the main action of a character. If the line of action is a smooth curve, the pose works well. If the line is angled, the pose looks awkward. Study the examples on these pages— good and bad. Notice that the good action lines have smooth curves that flow through the body without right angles or sudden changes in direction.

Correct! Here it really looks as if SpongeBob is kicking with all the power in his body because his body is leaning into the kick.

Oops! This pose is awkward because his body and leg aren't working together; the angle of his body doesn't show how much effort it really takes for his kick.

Correct! Here Patrick has two lines of action, which work together to emphasize his mood. His right arm and left leg follow one line of action. The curve of his body, from his head through his right leg, follows another.

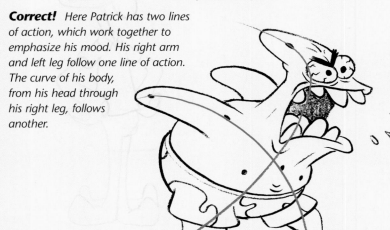

Oops! This line of action changes direction abruptly, so there's no energy here. Patrick still looks mad, but he's not going anywhere.

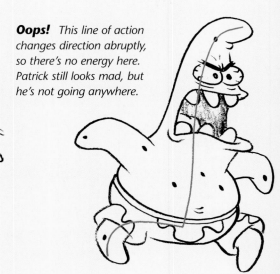

Correct! This pose has plenty of tension and energy. Notice that even the legs echo the curve of the body's action line.

Oops! The body parts aren't working together here—they actually seem to be working against each other!

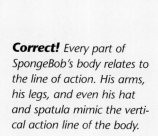

Correct! Every part of SpongeBob's body relates to the line of action. His arms, his legs, and even his hat and spatula mimic the vertical action line of the body.

Oops! This pose is much weaker because it doesn't have a true direction; notice that even the arms don't have much energy.

Testing the Line of Action

There's a simple way to test your line of action (and it doesn't involve a multiple-choice quiz). Place a piece of tracing paper over your sketch, and fill in the outline with pencil, making a silhouette of the character. If you can't immediately understand (or "read") the action as it appears in the silhouette, your drawing will need some fixin'!

Is your line of action working?

The silhouette will show!

13

Straight-Ahead Animation

In **straight-ahead** animation, the animator simply draws one pose after another, creating a sequence of growth or movement. Straight-ahead animation is best for creating simple actions that don't need a lot of planning, such as a character waving or a flower growing. With straight-ahead animation, the subject typically stays in place on the page, and movement occurs without drastic changes in between drawings. This example of SpongeBob jumping for joy is an example of straight-ahead animation.

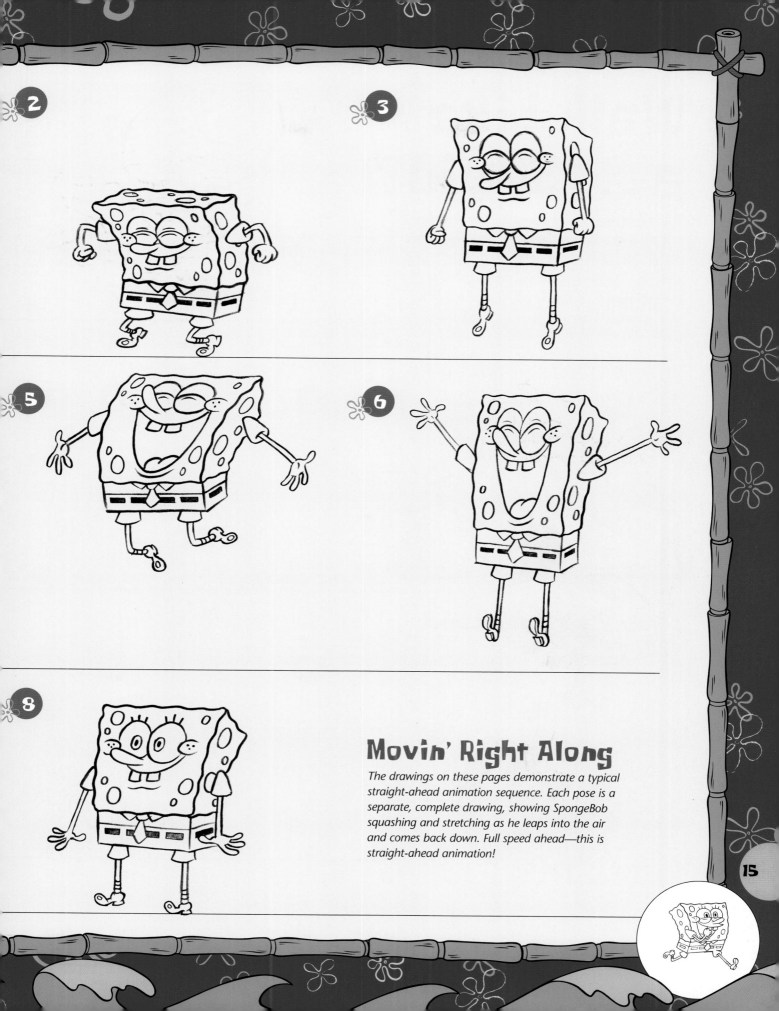

Movin' Right Along

The drawings on these pages demonstrate a typical straight-ahead animation sequence. Each pose is a separate, complete drawing, showing SpongeBob squashing and stretching as he leaps into the air and comes back down. Full speed ahead—this is straight-ahead animation!

Walk Like a . . . Squid?

Squidward may have 6 tentacles, but he walks just like a two-legged character, as shown in this 12-drawing demonstration of the straight-ahead technique. Drawing 1 follows drawing 12, so the action cycle can be repeated as many times as you want. When you have the basic cycle down, you can add other actions as well. For example, as Squidward walks, you can make him turn his head and smile or lift his arm and wave. Use your imagination!

TiP
Slower actions need more drawings to make them Flow smoothly!

Walk This Way

Animators draw on pieces of clear acetate, called **cels,** *which can be layered over one another. When a character cel is placed over the background cel, it looks as if they are all in the same drawing. With layered cels, there are two ways to make a character move past a background. With the* **straight-ahead** *approach, the character moves while the background stays still. With the* **panned** *approach, the character stays still while the background moves.*

Straight-Ahead

When a character just changes position, the background doesn't need to change at all. Here each step takes Squidward farther to the right, while the background stays in place. If you kept drawing this sequence, eventually Squidward would walk off the edge of the page!

Panned

Here Squidward appears to take many steps but actually stays in place. Instead the background is pulled—or panned—behind him, so Squidward seems to be moving forward.

Extremes and in-Betweens

In **pose-planning,** an animator draws the **extremes** of an action (the actual expression or pose, also called the "key drawings") and then adds **in-betweens** to connect the movement from one extreme to the next. The in-betweens are as necessary to animation as, well, water is to a sea sponge!

Here Patrick goes from deep thought to "a-ha." His facial expression can't just jump from one emotion to the next—the in-between smooths the transition by showing the stages of the change.

Extreme   in-Between   Extreme

Here Mr. Krabs transitions from "near boiling" to "steamed." The in-between shows the changes in his eyelids, mouth, and claws in progress.

Extreme   in-Between   Extreme

What's the Plan?

Animators are very imaginative folks, but even they don't just start drawing without a plan in hand. Before you dive right into animating your scene, think about the action you're going to draw. Then roughly sketch— or scribble!—the basic poses in the order in which you think they should happen. Now take a sec to see if the scene works as planned. Don't throw in the spatula if you have to make changes—since you're working with sketches, you can easily change anything that doesn't fit the action. Now move forward with your plan!

Here the idea is to get SpongeBob to flip the Krabby Patty into his mouth. First he must flip the Patty up in the air.

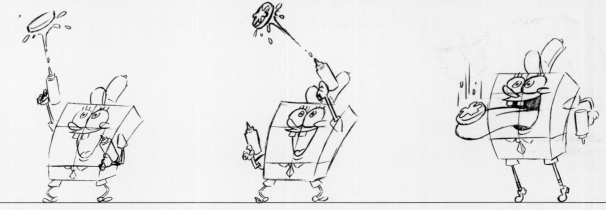

Next he'll squirt the Patty in the air with condiments and then catch it on his tongue.

In the end, we'll let him happily munch away.

JellyFishin'

Pose-planning animation is great for dramatic actions—like SpongeBob trying to catch jellyfish! In this 8-drawing example of pose-planning, a jellyfish catches SpongeBob's attention (Extreme 1), and he crouches down to anticipate the jump (Extreme 2). He leaps up into the air (Extreme 3), takes a swipe at the jellyfish (Extreme 4), and then he returns to secure footing on the sandy ocean floor (Extreme 5). The major in-betweens here show how the gesture and movement are developed.

1

Extreme
pose 1

2

Extreme
pose 2

5

in-between
pose

6

Extreme
pose 4

3 in-between pose

4 Extreme pose 3

7 in-between pose

8 Extreme pose 5

SpongeBob Marathon

This 12-drawing cycle shows SpongeBob on the run. The more drawings in a run cycle, the slower the action. In a faster run cycle (say, one with 8 drawings), SpongeBob would probably lean forward more to show the effort of his action—and his speed. This cycle uses pose-planning animation and a special kind of "extreme," called a "contact drawing." Drawings 1 and 5 are contact drawings because each one is the first drawing in each stride where the foot touches the ground. The contact drawings are always placed first, and then the rest of the in-between actions are built around them.

Speedy Sponge

When you want to make an action appear fast, you use fewer drawings in your cycle. So if you want to make an action **really** fast, it makes sense to simply cut out even more steps, right? Absolutely! But when you make your action very fast, it can be hard for the viewer to grasp the full effect. The solution? Speed lines! Speed lines are light, trailing lines that help the eye follow a quick action. The speed lines appear only when the action is taking place, disappearing as soon as the action is complete.

4

8

Line 'em Up!
For a sudden burst of movement, kick up a cloud of dust behind a character's speed lines. (In Bikini Bottom, use bubbles!) You can pair squash and stretch with speed lines too; the oval-shaped baseball and bubbles work with the lines to show speed.

23

Two-For-One!

For every second of a cartoon, the animation team has to create 24 drawings—so it's no surprise that animators have discovered a few shortcuts to limit the amount of work they have to do! With **limited animation,** you redraw only the parts you want to change. So rather than starting a brand new drawing every time, you can "hold" a basic pose for several frames as you change other features on a different layer, or cel (see page 17)—creating many slightly different drawings. The examples of Patrick below show three very different emotions, all using one body pose.

Here's a basic drawing of Patrick's body. This pose can be used for many different actions.

Draw arms and facial features on a separate layer. When placed over the body, they convey the emotion.

Paired with the first drawing, Patrick's contented expression and relaxed arms show his happy-go-lucky nature.

Drawing his arms in a different position and giving him a toothy grin makes Patrick appear sly and confident—without any changes to the first drawing underneath.

Here Patrick seems angry. It's the clenched fists, closed eyes, and downturned mouth that convey this emotion.

Animators also sometimes use **cutouts,** a special kind of limited animation. Cutouts can be hands, clothes, mouths, or any piece that's drawn separately and then placed over a basic body pose drawing. The cutouts can be used over and over again, just as a basic body pose can be. And individual parts can be used in any number of combinations, saving time. (And, as Mr. Krabs knows, saving time means saving money!)

Begin with a simple pose.

Then draw the features on separate sheets so you can change SpongeBob's expression quickly and easily. Cutouts can be reused as many times as you need to repeat an expression!

Layer the cutouts over the body pose, and changing SpongeBob's silly expression becomes a snap!

25

These two examples use the same basic body pose, but on the left SpongeBob is running for joy, and on the right he's ready to rumble. Swapping facial expressions and adding a helmet and gloves give an entirely new meaning to the pose!

Board For the Un-Bored

Ahoy, mates! Now that you know the basics of animation, what's next? Real animators begin with a story before they begin sketching. They plan the action by using a **storyboard,** or a series of sketched scenes that show the basic progression of the script. The storyboard breaks down the story into a series of frames, the way a comic strip does. When they begin with a storyboard, animators don't waste valuable time on sketches they won't use; they can work out any problems with the script before they begin drawing the action cycles. Check out this storyboard to get a feel for how it works, and then try creating one of your own!

Scene 19

[Dialogue] SB: What!? What did you say?

Scene 22

[Dialogue] SQ (yells): I've never had a Krabby Patty! I've never had a Krabby Patty! I've never had a Krabby Patty!

Once Upon A Time . . .

This a real storyboard, drawn by a professional SpongeBob SquarePants animator! Here the animator has roughly illustrated the script by sketching out each important situation in the story in a separate frame, making notes about the action and dialogue in each frame. The animator looks at the frames individually to be sure they make sense together. The storyboard is approved when all the scenes of the cartoon are working according to plan; then the animators can begin drawing.

Scene 24C

[Action] Camera pans over slightly as SB runs around boat.
[Dialogue] SB: . . . you're always so miserable!

26

Scene 20

[Dialogue] SQ: I said I've never had a Krabby Patty.

Scene 21A

[Action] SB is stunned for a beat.

Scene 21B

[Action] SB lifts up a dictionary and glasses from behind the stove.
[Dialogue] SB: Those words! Is it possible to use them in a sentence together like that?

Scene 23

[Dialogue] SB: NEVER HAD A KRABBY PATTY?!! Well, you've gotta have one right now before something bad happens!

Scene 24A

[Action] Start pose

Scene 24B

[Action] SB bursts through door carrying a Krabby Patty.
[Dialogue] SB: No wonder . . .

cene 24D

[Dialogue] SB: Here, try this!

Scene 25A

[Dialogue] SQ: Try one of those radioactive sludge balls you call food?!

Scene 25B

[Dialogue] SQ: Next I suppose you'll want me to go square dancing with Patrick.

Flip Book Frolic

Another essential part of the animation process is testing the action cycles. Before filling in all the details of the final sketches, animators use a flip book to do a pencil test. They place one step of the cycle on each page of the flip book, then thumb through the book to watch the drawings move as if they were on film. You can make your own flip book just like a professional animator's by following the directions on these pages.

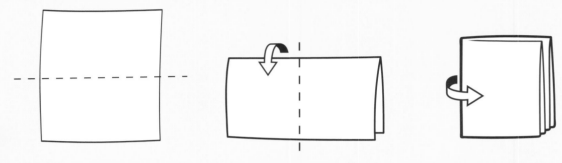

1

Your flip book should be made of lightweight paper, which will make it easy to see through the top drawing to the drawings below. Start by folding a piece of paper in half, then in half again. Make four of these.

2

Now stack the four folded pieces as shown. Keep all the folded edges together.

3

Staple all the pages 3 or 4 times along the narrow folded edges.

4

Trim off the longer folded edges with a pair of scissors. (You may need an adult's help for this part.)

5

Wrap a piece of masking tape around the flip book to cover the staples. This will make the book more comfortable to handle.

6

Now start drawing! It is easier to begin with the last page of the flip book and work toward the front. This way you can refer to the drawing underneath when sketching the next step, which makes it easier to keep your SpongeBob characters consistent. If you start from the back, be sure to begin with the first step of the cycle so the action doesn't go backward.

7

Be sure to place your drawings in the same spot (toward the right-hand side) of each page, so you can see the action as you flip.

8

Ask an adult to evenly trim the edges of the flip book with a craft knife to make the pages easier to flip.

9

To view the action, hold the flip book at the spine, and quickly flip the pages from back to front. And you're ready for action!

Zoetrope Fun

A **zoetrope** is a nifty way to test your new animation skills. It creates the illusion of movement, similar to the way a flip book does—except instead of flipping, you spin! To make your own zoetrope, use a photocopier to enlarge the patterns on page 31 to 110%; then copy them onto heavy paper or card stock, and carefully trim out each piece. (Note: You will need to make two copies each of the Animation Strip and the Zoetrope Side.)

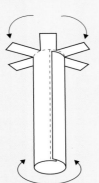

 1

Cut the tabs at the top of the handle. Roll the handle into a tube, and fasten it with tape or glue. Fold the tabs down as shown.

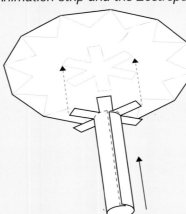

 2

Line up the tabs with the template on the base, and tape or glue the handle in place. Make sure it's secure so your zoetrope will spin really well.

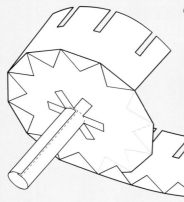

 3

Fasten the two side pieces into one long strip. Fold up the triangle tabs, and tape or glue them into place around the bottom of the base. Fasten the ends together.

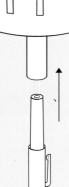

 4

Fasten the two animation strips together with tape, and then draw an action cycle of SpongeBob or another character on the strip. Next place it inside the zoetrope. The pictures should fit completely below the slots, and each image should be centered under a slot.

5

Place a flat-ended pen, pencil, or wooden dowel in the handle, and hold the dowel below the handle. Now spin the zoetrope, and watch the action through the slots. The characters inside appear to move! Tip: The effect works best if your face is close to the zoetrope and you hold it near a light source (such as a lamp).

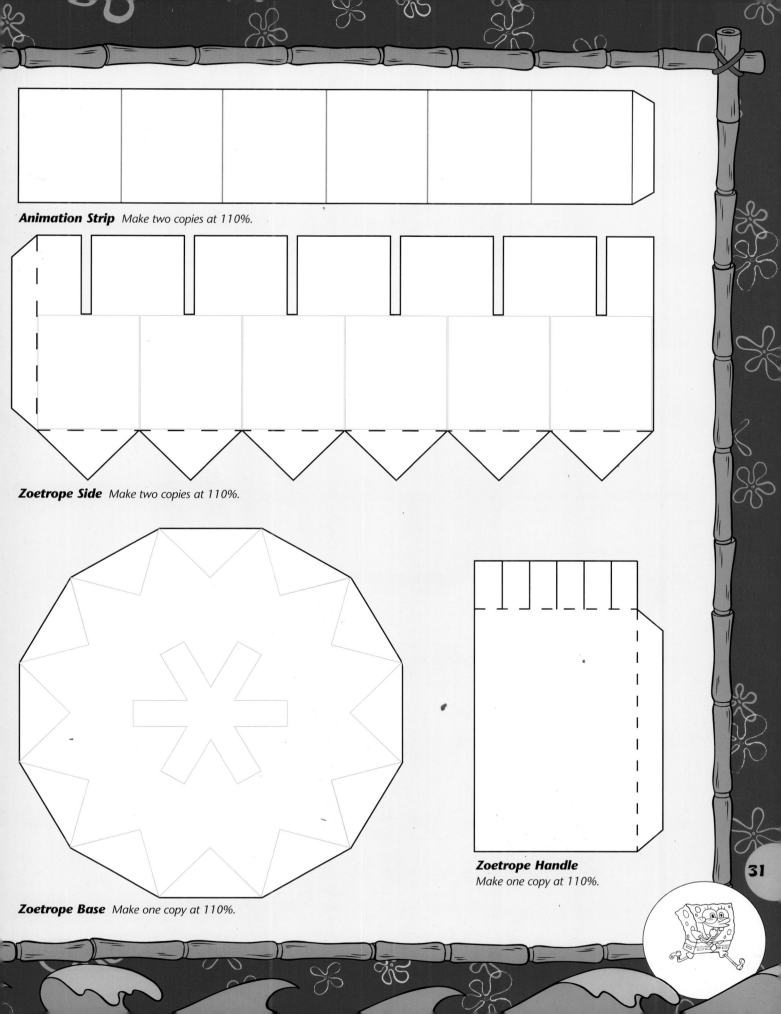

Animation Strip *Make two copies at 110%.*

Zoetrope Side *Make two copies at 110%.*

Zoetrope Base *Make one copy at 110%.*

Zoetrope Handle
Make one copy at 110%.

31

Sailorific Tips

- When drawing a cycle, always work in pencil, leaving out the details until you are sure the action works.

- Use a light box; it's a useful tool for making character movement consistent.

- Practice drawing your characters from all angles and in every position before you begin animating. (Refer to Walter Foster Publishing's book **How to Draw Nickelodeon's SpongeBob SquarePants**™ for complete drawing instructions!)

- Keep your drawings consistent. Trace them if necessary, altering only the parts that change with the action.

- Study different facial expressions. Use a mirror to practice and test new expressions on yourself.

- Remember that in-between poses are used to smooth the action—but they also slow it down.

- Always start with an action line to establish your character's pose—and to check for proper balance.

- Keep it simple. Don't try to do too much right away. Just be patient and stick with it!

- Remember that animators always learn from their mistakes. If you try to animate a walk and it turns out looking like a limp, that's okay! That just means you've discovered how to animate a limp!

- Practice, practice, practice. The more you draw, the better an animator you'll be. If you draw every day, you'll start to notice huge improvements in your work.

- Most important: Have a spongerifically good time!